NATURE'S SUPERHEROES

SUPER COCKROACHES

by Karen Latchana Kenney

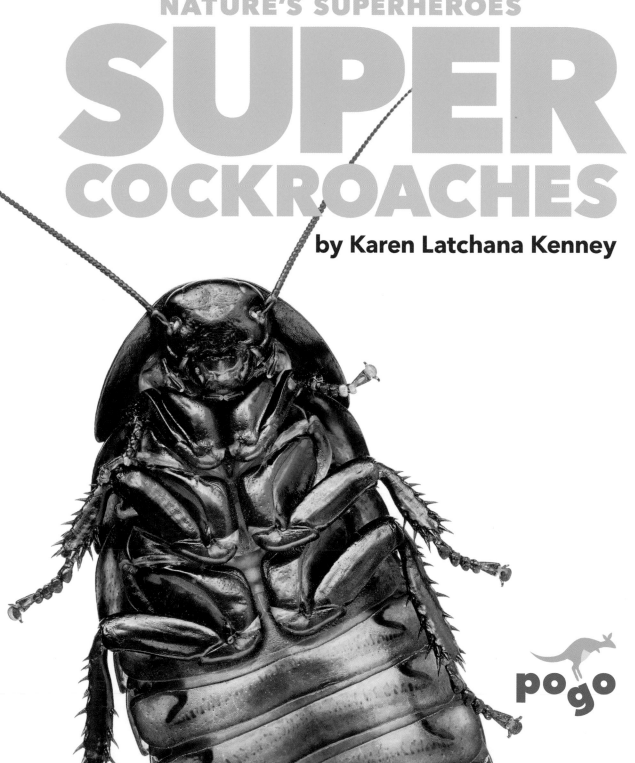

pogo

Ideas for Parents and Teachers

Pogo Books let children practice reading informational text while introducing them to nonfiction features such as headings, labels, sidebars, maps, and diagrams, as well as a table of contents, glossary, and index.

Carefully leveled text with a strong photo match offers early fluent readers the support they need to succeed.

Before Reading

- "Walk" through the book and point out the various nonfiction features. Ask the student what purpose each feature serves.
- Look at the glossary together. Read and discuss the words.

Read the Book

- Have the child read the book independently.
- Invite him or her to list questions that arise from reading.

After Reading

- Discuss the child's questions. Talk about how he or she might find answers to those questions.
- Prompt the child to think more. Ask: What did you know about cockroaches before you read this book? What more do you want to learn after reading it?

Pogo Books are published by Jump!
5357 Penn Avenue South
Minneapolis, MN 55419
www.jumplibrary.com

Copyright © 2018 Jump!
International copyright reserved in all countries.
No part of this book may be reproduced in any form without written permission from the publisher.

Library of Congress Cataloging-in-Publication Data

Names: Kenney, Karen Latchana, author.
Title: Super cockroaches / by Karen Latchana Kenney.
Description: Minneapolis, MN: Jump!, Inc., [2018]
Series: Nature's superheroes | Audience: Ages 7-10.
Identifiers: LCCN 2017029890 (print)
LCCN 2017030256 (ebook)
ISBN 9781624967085 (ebook)
ISBN 9781620319697 (hardcover: alk. paper)
ISBN 9781620319703 (pbk.)
Subjects: LCSH: Cockroaches–Juvenile literature.
Adaptation (Biology)–Juvenile literature.
Classification: LCC QL505.5 (ebook)
LCC QL505.5 .K46 2017 (print) | DDC 595.7/28–dc23
LC record available at https://lccn.loc.gov/2017029890

Editor: Jenna Trnka
Book Designer: Michelle Sonnek
Photo Researcher: Michelle Sonnek

Photo Credits: jamlong tunkaew/Shutterstock, cover; skydie/Shutterstock, 1; PK.Phuket studio/Shutterstock, 3; Prachaya Roekdeethaweesab/Shutterstock, 4; Prachaya Roekdeethaweesab/Shutterstock, 5; Prachaya Roekdeethaweesab/Shutterstock, 6-7; Susan Schmitz/Shutterstock, 8; kurt_G/Shutterstock, 9; H. Bellmann/F. Hecker/Age Fotostock, 10-11; mansum008/iStock, 12-13; Illg, Gordon & Cathy/Animals Animals, 14-15; Natural History Museum/Alamy, 16; Wisanu_nuu/Shutterstock, 17; Somchai Som/Shutterstock, 18-19 (cockroach); klosfoto/iStock, 18-19 (glue); blickwinkel/Alamy, 20-21; ittipon/Shutterstock, 23.

Printed in the United States of America at Corporate Graphics in North Mankato, Minnesota.

TABLE OF CONTENTS

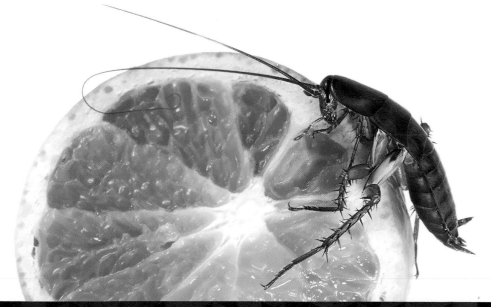

CHAPTER 1

INCREDIBLE INSECTS

What can squish its body flat to fit into tight spaces? What is almost impossible to crush? And what can live a week without its head?

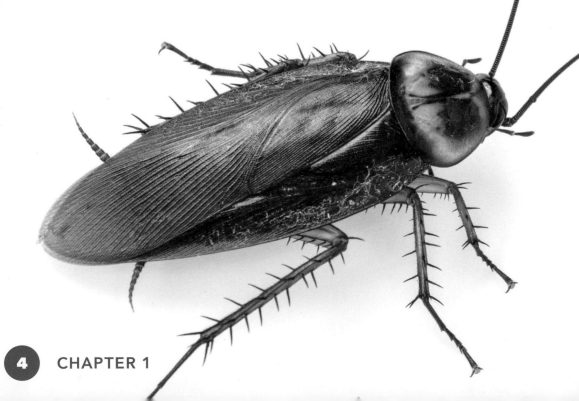

Not many people like them. They are small. But they have some huge powers. They are cockroaches!

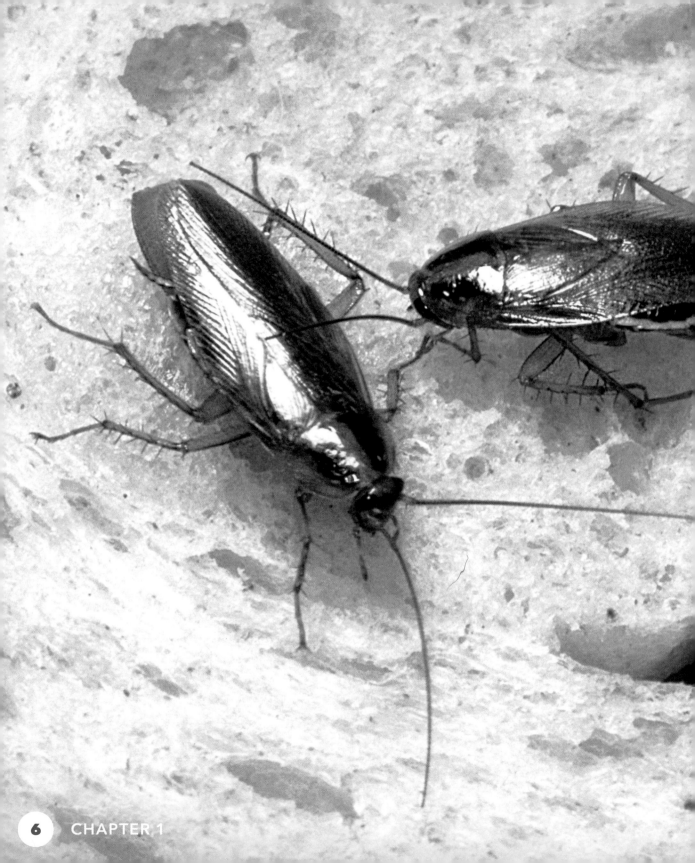

Close to 4,000 kinds of cockroaches live around the world. The small German cockroach is the most common kind found in homes. These cockroaches are pests. They eat any food they find.

Many cockroaches live together in a **colony**. They **breed** quickly. A German cockroach colony can have 10,000 babies in one year!

DID YOU KNOW?

The largest cockroach is the rhinoceros cockroach. It can weigh as much as a parakeet!

CHAPTER 2

SUPERHERO POWERS

Cockroaches scurry. They escape into tiny spaces. How? They make their bodies flat!

A cockroach can do this because of its **exoskeleton**. This is a skeleton on the outside of its body. It has plates. They bend.

plates

The cockroach can shrink half its height in less than one second! That lets it crawl under doors and into cracks.

What else helps cockroaches escape? They are fast. To run, they stand up on their back legs. Then they quickly scurry long distances.

DID YOU KNOW?

Cockroaches can travel the length of a bicycle in just one second!

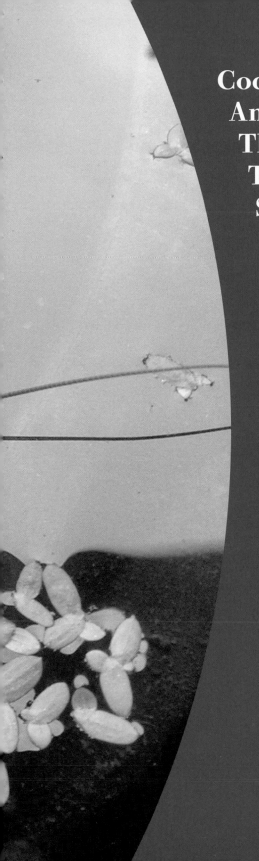

Cockroaches love **damp** places.
And they are expert swimmers.
Their bodies float in water.
They can hold their breath, too.
Some cockroaches can hold
their breath for 40 minutes!

The Madagascar hissing cockroach has a different kind of superpower. It hisses. It does this to sound like a snake. It pushes air out of breathing holes on its **abdomen**. This makes a hissing sound. It is loud. It scares away **predators**. It also attracts **mates**.

TAKE A LOOK!

A cockroach has many features that make it one of nature's superheroes!

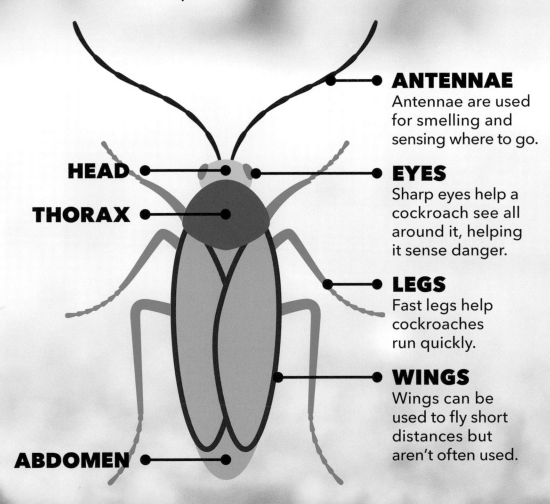

HEAD

THORAX

ABDOMEN

ANTENNAE
Antennae are used for smelling and sensing where to go.

EYES
Sharp eyes help a cockroach see all around it, helping it sense danger.

LEGS
Fast legs help cockroaches run quickly.

WINGS
Wings can be used to fly short distances but aren't often used.

CHAPTER 3

SUPER SURVIVORS

Cockroaches have been around since before the dinosaurs. We know this because scientists have found cockroach **fossils**. How have they **survived** so long?

fossil ····▶

They cannot be crushed easily. They can handle 900 times their own weight on top of them. Wow!

They **adapt**. A cockroach can go a month without eating. Cockroaches in the wild eat food found in nature. Plants, fruit, and dead insects. But ones that live in homes eat almost anything. Soap? Yes. Glue? Sure! They have stomachs of steel.

A cockroach can even survive a whole week without its head! This is because it does not need a head to breathe. Cockroaches have tiny holes in their bodies. They breathe through them.

Cockroaches are experts at adapting. And they are almost **indestructible**. These powers have helped them survive many thousands of years.

DID YOU KNOW?

A cockroach will die after a week with no head. This is only because it needs a head to drink water. Cockroaches need water to survive.

MOVING EXOSKELETON

The plates of an exoskeleton connect at joints. This lets a bug move. Make an exoskeleton to see how it moves.

What You Need:
- file folder
- scissors
- ruler
- hole punch
- tape
- 4 paper fasteners

1. Cut the tab off the file folder. Then cut at the fold. Now you have two 8 x 12-inch (20 x 30-cm) pieces of card stock.

2. Cut each piece in half the long way.

3. Leave one strip as it is. Trim the other three strips. Make one 11 inches (28 cm) long. Make another 10 inches (25 cm) long. Make the third 9 inches (23 cm) long.

4. Tape the short ends of each strip together to make four tubes.

5. Punch one hole on the biggest tube. Put it one-half inch (1 cm) from the edge.

6. Punch two holes in the other tubes. Put them on the same side. Make one one-half inch (1 cm) from the bottom edge. Make the other one-half inch (1 cm) from the top edge.

7. Now connect the tubes. Line them up from biggest to smallest. Attach the tubes with the paper fasteners. Make them go through the holes. Ask an adult for help.

8. Slip the exoskeleton over your arm. Try moving your arm. Does the exoskeleton bend? Where does it bend?

GLOSSARY

abdomen: The back section of an insect's body.

adapt: To change to live in a new situation.

breed: To produce young.

colony: A large group of insects that lives together.

damp: Slightly wet.

exoskeleton: A bony structure on the outside of an animal.

fossils: The remains of animals or plants from millions of years ago, saved as rocks.

indestructible: Incapable of being destroyed or injured.

mates: Male and female partners of a pair of animals.

predators: Animals that hunt other animals for food.

survived: Continued to live.

INDEX

TO LEARN MORE

Learning more is as easy as 1, 2, 3.

1) Go to www.factsurfer.com

2) Enter "supercockroaches" into the search box.

3) Click the "Surf" button to see a list of websites.

With factsurfer, finding more information is just a click away.